CYBER THREATS

RANSOMWARE

by Connor Stratton

FOCUS READERS®
NAVIGATOR

WWW.FOCUSREADERS.COM

Copyright © 2026 by Focus Readers®, Mendota Heights, MN 55120. All rights reserved. No part of this book may be reproduced or utilized in any form or by any means without written permission from the publisher.

Focus Readers is distributed by North Star Editions:
sales@northstareditions.com | 888-417-0195

Produced for Focus Readers by Red Line Editorial.

Photographs ©: Shutterstock Images, cover, 1, 4–5, 7, 8–9, 11, 14–15, 16, 24, 26, 29; Red Line Editorial, 13; Ted S. Warren/AP Images, 19; Andrew Harnik/AP Images, 20–21; iStockphoto, 23

Library of Congress Cataloging-in-Publication Data
Library of Congress Cataloging-in-Publication Data is available on the Library of Congress website.

ISBN
979-8-88998-520-4 (hardcover)
979-8-88998-581-5 (ebook pdf)
979-8-88998-552-5 (hosted ebook)

Printed in the United States of America
Mankato, MN
082025

ABOUT THE AUTHOR
Connor Stratton writes and edits nonfiction children's books. He lives in Minnesota.

TABLE OF CONTENTS

CHAPTER 1
Taking Down a Pipeline 5

CHAPTER 2
How It Works 9

CHAPTER 3
Purpose and Impact 15

CHAPTER 4
Fighting Ransomware 21

CYBER SAFETY
Playing Your Part 28

Focus Questions • 30
Glossary • 31
To Learn More • 32
Index • 32

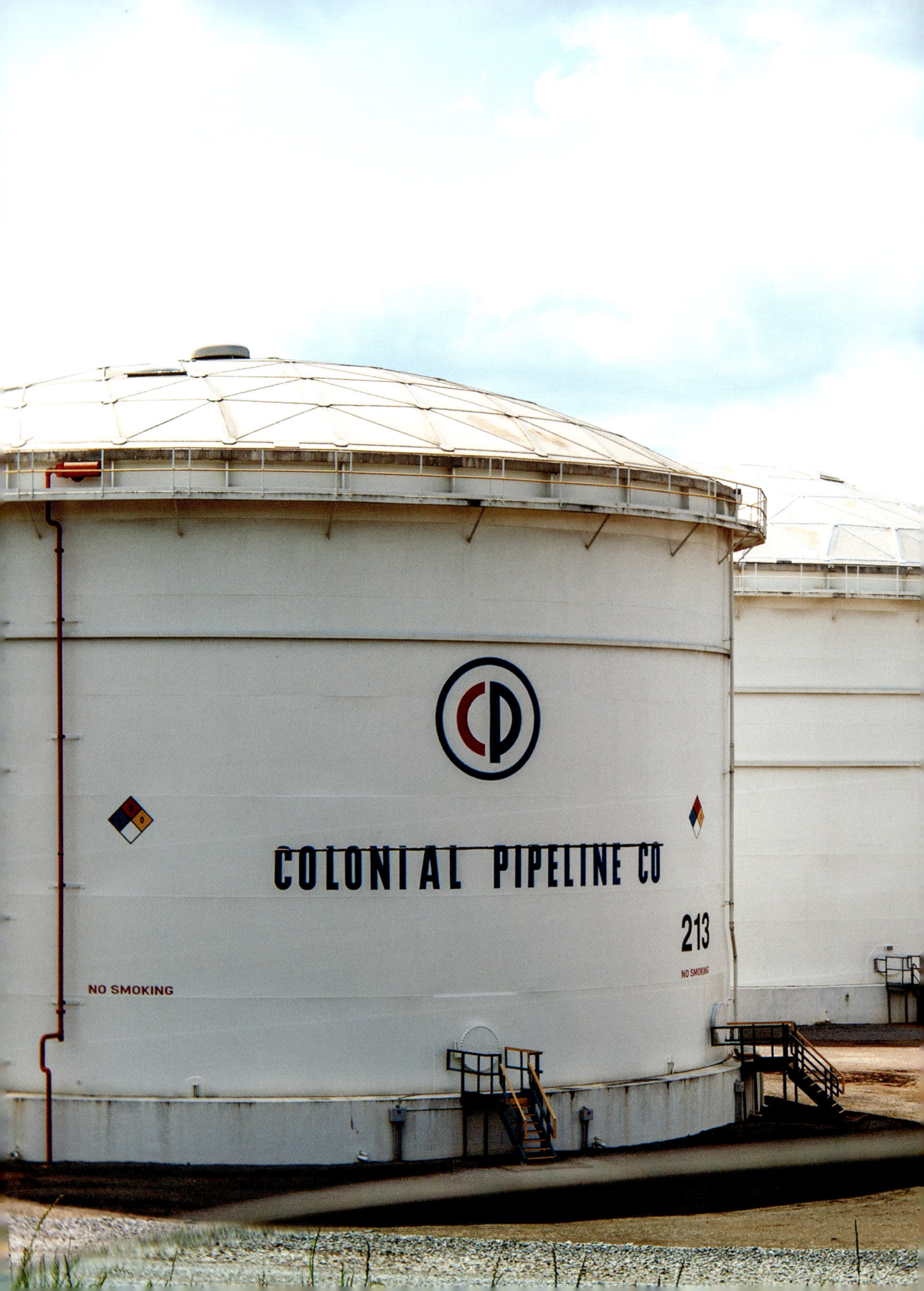
CP
COLONIAL PIPELINE CO
213
NO SMOKING
NO SMOKING

CHAPTER 1

TAKING DOWN A PIPELINE

In May 2021, **hackers** launched a major cyberattack. They targeted Colonial Pipeline. This company provided gasoline and jet fuel to millions of Americans.

Colonial Pipeline did not use **two-factor authentication**. So, the hackers needed just one password. They got the password, which gave

> In the early 2020s, more than 50 million people depended on Colonial Pipeline for gasoline.

5

them access to the company's **network**. Then the hackers used ransomware. This software shut down part of the network. The hackers demanded money from the company to stop the attack.

    The company's leaders were worried. The attack had messed up their billing system. And they thought it could harm more of the network. So, the company shut down its entire gasoline pipeline. Suddenly, thousands of gas stations did not have enough fuel. Gas prices went up, too.

    Eventually, Colonial Pipeline paid the hackers. The hackers received nearly $5 million. Then, the company reopened

Nearly 17,000 gas stations ran out of fuel after the cyberattack on Colonial Pipeline.

the pipeline. Later, the US government helped the company get some of the money back. But the crisis was a shocking lesson. Cyberattacks could take down key **infrastructure**. And society was not yet prepared to respond.

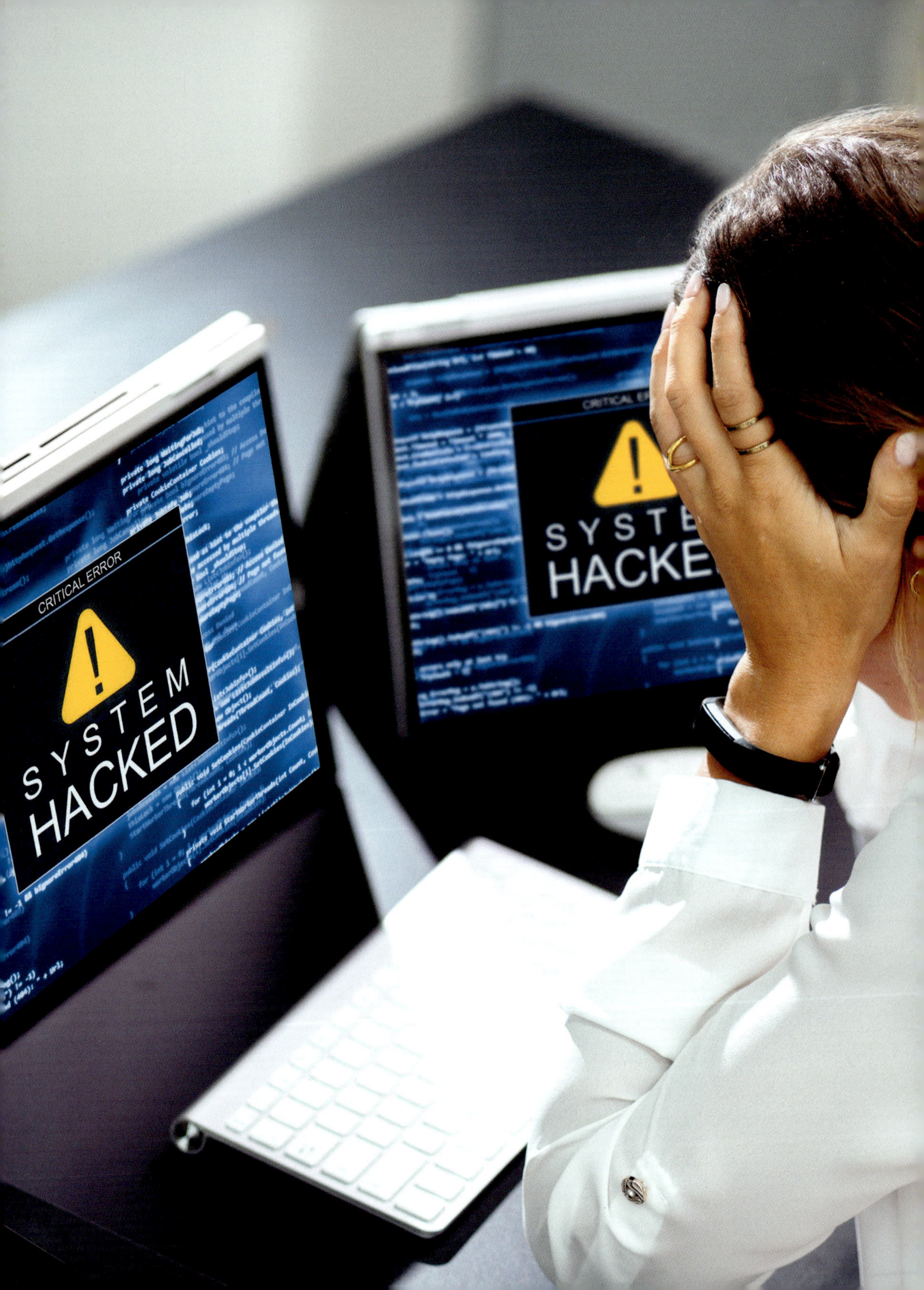
CRITICAL ERROR
SYSTEM
HACKED

CHAPTER 2

HOW IT WORKS

Software is a set of computer instructions. It tells a computer how to run. Software that is made to have negative effects is called malware. Ransomware is one type of malware. It locks a computer or its data. Then it sends a message to the victim. The message says that the victim must pay

> *Malware* comes from the phrase "malicious software." *Malicious* means "intended to do harm."

money to regain access. Paying money in this way is called a ransom.

Hackers use several different types of ransomware. The most common is crypto-ransomware. This type locks important data on computers. However, victims can still use their devices. They can see what data is locked. Locker ransomware is also common. This type stops people from using their computers at all.

Ransomware attacks start by gaining access to a victim's computer. To do so, many hackers use phishing. That's when hackers trick people into giving up personal information or passwords.

Ransomware programs use complex software. It would take a powerful computer years to unlock files.

For example, a hacker may send a fake bank email. The email tells the person to confirm their account password. The person may enter it. Then the hacker can log in to their account. They install the ransomware. Hackers could also gain access with fake links. When a victim clicks, the ransomware starts installing.

After installation, ransomware uses **encryption** software. Encryption uses an **algorithm** to make the computer's data unreadable. Often, only a digital key can

CRYPTOCURRENCY

Most ransomware attackers ask for money in **cryptocurrency**. This form of payment is easy to send across countries. So, hackers can target people all around the world. In addition, crypto transactions are hard to reverse. That makes it difficult for victims to get their money back. Some hackers also think crypto can't be tracked. However, law enforcement often can track it.

undo the algorithm. Hackers keep the key. If victims pay the ransom, hackers may share the key.

STEPS OF RANSOMWARE ATTACKS

1. Hacker gains access to device.
2. Hacker uses encryption to lock data.
3. Hacker asks victim for money.
4. Victim pays money to hacker.
5. Hacker gives encryption key to victim.
6. Victim can use device again.

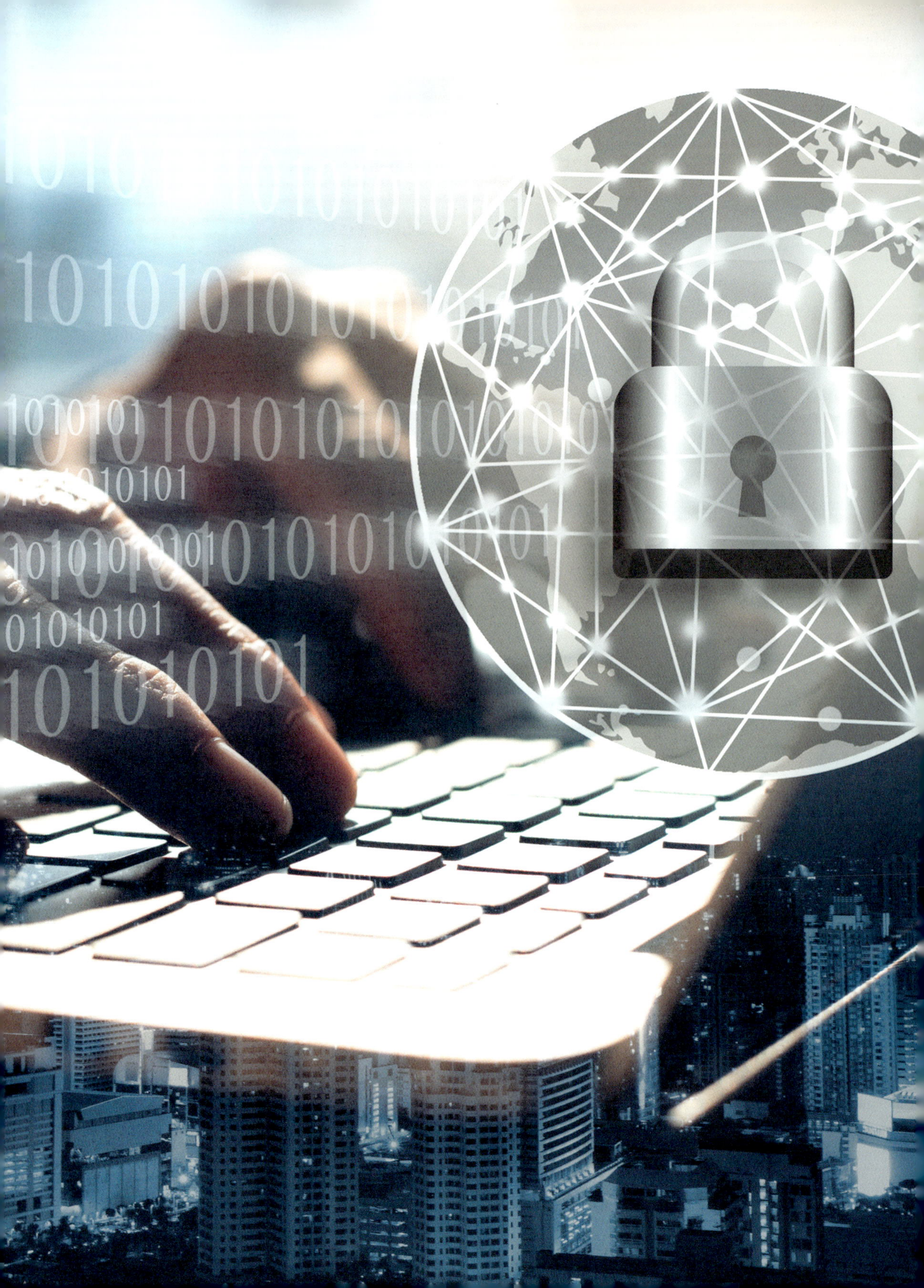

CHAPTER 3

PURPOSE AND IMPACT

Hackers use ransomware attacks for several reasons. Sometimes hackers want to cause chaos. In 2017, for example, hackers used ransomware called WannaCry. The WannaCry attack was huge. It hit hundreds of thousands of computers. However, the hackers asked

The 2017 WannaCry attack affected devices in more than 150 countries.

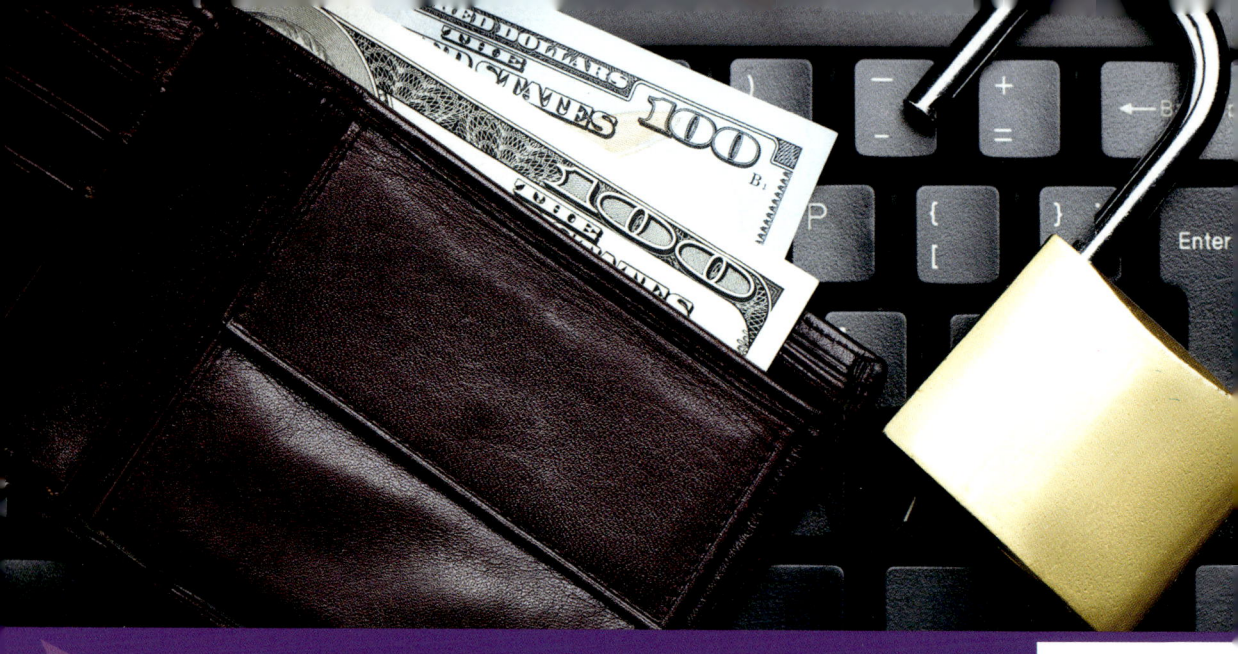

In 2023, payments from ransomware attacks topped $1 billion for the first time.

for only $300 in ransom. Their main goal was to cause panic.

Most often, the goal of a ransomware attack is money. Hackers try to force their victims to pay large amounts. That's why hackers often focus on big companies or parts of governments. Those groups can afford high ransoms. In addition, these groups may have a wide reach. Hospitals are one example. If a hospital shuts down, many people could get sicker or die. So, hospitals under attack may choose to pay ransoms, even high ones.

Hackers often develop new approaches. For instance, more hackers have started

THE FIRST DEATH

In 2020, hackers attacked a hospital in Germany with ransomware. The hospital's computers shut down. A nearby woman required emergency care. Doctors at that hospital needed computer access to help her. As a result, paramedics could not bring the patient there. Instead, they drove her to a hospital miles away. However, the patient died on the way. It was the first death directly linked to ransomware.

using leakware. Leakware does not simply lock a victim's data. It also threatens to share the data. Banks store private information from many people. Laws require banks to protect that information. So, hackers often use leakware on bank networks. They aim to make more money on ransoms.

The risks of ransomware are increasing. Ransomware-as-a-service (RaaS) is one reason. With RaaS, people can hire hackers to do ransomware attacks. As a result, more people can launch attacks. They do not have to be computer experts.

The costs of ransomware are high. People may lose large amounts of

In 2019, the company Travelex faced a ransomware attack. It later went out of business.

money. They may lose important files. In addition, companies face disruption to their work. Ransomware attacks can even affect how customers see a company. People may lose trust. They may start using another business instead. Then the company may lose even more money.

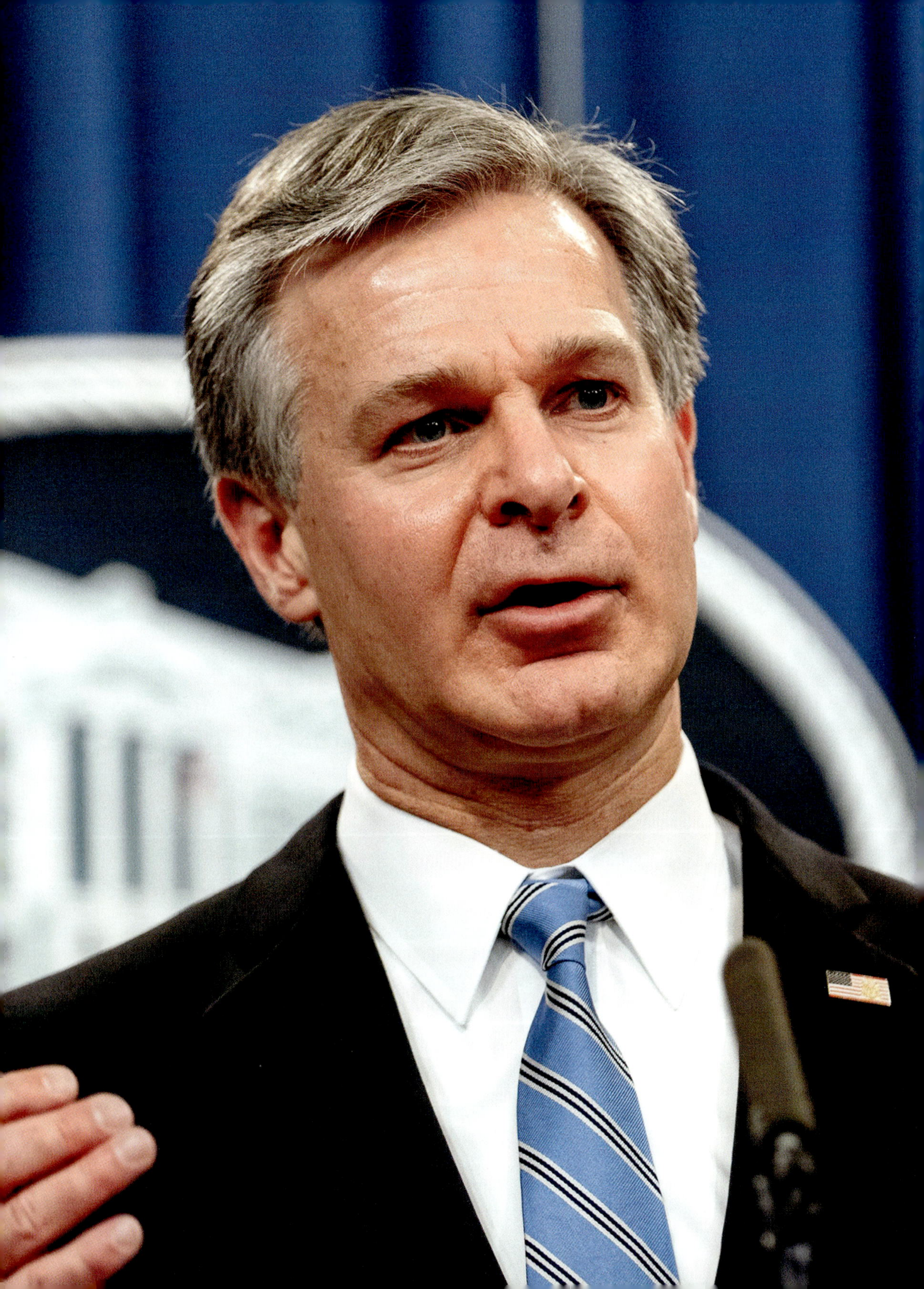

CHAPTER 4

FIGHTING RANSOMWARE

Ransomware attacks are a major threat. But many people are working hard to help. People in law enforcement take several actions. Law enforcement officials try to catch the hackers behind ransomware attacks. Officials also give advice about responding to attacks. For example, they say victims should not

In 2021, the FBI director spoke about resisting ransomware attacks at a press conference.

21

pay ransoms. Officials argue that paying the hackers may not even work. That's because hackers often just take the money. They leave the data locked.

Improving cybersecurity is another way to fight ransomware. People are developing stronger software to protect devices. For example, some companies work on antivirus programs. Better programs can find attacks much earlier.

Antivirus programs use several tools to detect attacks. Some scan a group's computers more often. They track normal behavior on the network. Then the programs can spot unusual behavior. That may point to an attack happening.

Bees are attracted to sweet things such as honey. That's how the honeypot method got its name. It uses a fake network to attract and trick hackers.

Another tool is called the honeypot method. That's when a group creates a fake computer network. Hackers try to break in. They launch a ransomware attack. The group's real network stays safe. But the attack gives the group information. They can prepare their real network for future attacks.

Ransomware protection programs send users alerts when they find something unusual.

Artificial intelligence (AI) programs can also help. These programs study lots of ransomware attacks. They find patterns in those attacks. Then they watch for those patterns on people's networks. When a pattern appears, AI programs send alerts. They let users know that ransomware may be present.

That helps people respond quickly. People may even be able to block the worst results. For example, some ransomware programs store the key in their code. After an attack finishes, the key is locked away. But while an attack is happening, some programs can find the key. Then, people can unlock their data.

Other software helps after ransomware attacks. Some programs create a new file whenever a file is changed. The old versions are kept separately. So, ransomware can't touch the original files. It just makes new versions that are encrypted. Later, people can delete those files. They can recover the originals.

Companies may hold cybersecurity trainings when they start using new software.

Educating users about ransomware is also important. To launch an attack, hackers need access to a computer system. That mainly happens when people give out too much information. For that reason, many companies and schools hold trainings. They teach people about ransomware threats. People also learn about phishing attacks. They can

26

learn how to keep their computers as safe as possible. That way, people are prepared, and fewer ransomware attacks happen in the first place.

TARGETING SCHOOLS

In 2023, hackers launched a ransomware attack against schools in Tucson, Arizona. The schools' computers all shut down. Then, school printers started printing ransom notes. The hackers demanded money. Without it, they would leak students' private information. School leaders decided not to pay. But the attack did have an effect. The school had to close for two weeks. This attack was part of a trend. As a result, the US government began focusing on cybersecurity in schools.

> CYBER SAFETY

PLAYING YOUR PART

Everyone can help protect against ransomware attacks. An easy method is updating computers often. That removes mistakes in programs that hackers can use.

Backing up files is another good step. When data is backed up, files are saved on a separate system. Then, if ransomware attacks happen, the files are still safe. People should do new backups often. That keeps the most-recent files saved.

Protecting access to computers is important, too. People should use two-factor authentication. They should also create strong passwords. Strong passwords include many letters, numbers, and symbols. Not repeating passwords is helpful, too.

In addition, people should be aware of common signs of phishing. For example, phishing

People can check whether antivirus software is installed on their computers.

messages often use strong language, such as "Act Now." People should think twice before clicking links in messages. And they should avoid offering personal information online. These steps can help keep computers safe and secure.

FOCUS QUESTIONS

Write your answers on a separate piece of paper.

1. Write a paragraph explaining why phishing is a common part of ransomware attacks.

2. What steps could you take to guard against ransomware?

3. What is the most common type of ransomware attack?
   - **A.** crypto-ransomware
   - **B.** locker ransomware
   - **C.** WannaCry attack

4. How does backing up data help protect against ransomware attacks?
   - **A.** It lets people buy new data that ransomware creates.
   - **B.** It stops ransomware from leaking private information.
   - **C.** It makes separate copies of files.

Answer key on page 32.

GLOSSARY

algorithm
A set of steps that a computer follows to complete a process.

artificial intelligence
The ability of a machine to make decisions on its own.

cryptocurrency
A money system that is digital and not controlled by a major bank or government.

encryption
The process of putting messages, information, or data into a secret code so that they cannot be understood by others.

hackers
People who illegally gain access to information on computer systems.

infrastructure
The systems, such as roads, water supplies, and energy distribution, that a region needs to function.

network
A system of computers and devices that are connected to one another.

two-factor authentication
Requiring two methods to access an account. It often involves a password and another device.

TO LEARN MORE

BOOKS

Chandler, Matt. *Cryptocurrency*. Focus Readers, 2022.
London, Martha. *Cybersecurity*. Bearport Publishing, 2023.
O'Sullivan, J. K. *Online Scams*. BrightPoint Press, 2022.

NOTE TO EDUCATORS

Visit **www.focusreaders.com** to find lesson plans, activities, links, and other resources related to this title.

INDEX

algorithm, 12–13
antivirus programs, 22
artificial intelligence (AI), 24

Colonial Pipeline, 5–7
cryptocurrency, 12
crypto-ransomware, 10
cybersecurity, 22, 27

governments, 7, 16, 27

hackers, 5–6, 10–13, 15–18, 21–23, 26–27, 28

honeypot method, 23

law enforcement, 12, 21
leakware, 18
locker ransomware, 10

malware, 9

networks, 6, 18, 22–24

passwords, 5, 10–11, 28
phishing, 10, 26, 28–29

programs, 22, 24–25, 28

ransomware-as-a-service (RaaS), 18

software, 6, 9, 12, 22, 25

two-factor authentication, 5, 28

WannaCry, 15–16

Answer Key: 1. Answers will vary; 2. Answers will vary; 3. A; 4. C